Strength to Climb the Mountains

Margaret Harrison

All Scripture verses are from the Holy Bible, King James Version

To purchase additional copies of this book contact Margaret Harrison at:

1141 Hoots Road, Yadkinville, North Carolina 27055

Whitline Ink Incorporated   PO Box 668, 114 S. Carolina Avenue, Boonville, North Carolina 27011
whitlineink@yadtel.net   (336) 367-6914

Dedicated to my sister-in-law Donna Harrison
for her unlimited love and support,
and to Roseleen Brandon and Connie Key,
who graciously proofed my manuscript.

Foreword

None of us can ever be certain of what we will face in any given day of our lives. Just as the weather can change from sunny to cloudy or from hot to cold, circumstances day to day can quickly change. The Harrison family encountered a crisis situation September 9, 1997. A parent's worst nightmare: a phone call…news none of us would ever want to hear…"your son has been involved in an automobile accident." This is the first-hand account written from the pen of a mother of how the grace of God and the power of prayer *can* and *does* make a difference in real life situations. As Margaret walks us through the daily struggles that she and her husband faced as they held on to hope while Preston fought for his life, I know you will be moved. You will learn. You will weep. You will rejoice with the Harrisons as their son begins to recover and faith is rewarded.

I am privileged to be called Pastor and often times witness the truths of God's Word played out on the stage of life by people who put them to the test and find validity in those promises. Truly our God is "greater than any need, bigger than any problem." Get ready to embark on an "adventure in faith" as you read.

Pastor Bruce Freeman
Peace Haven Baptist Church
Yadkinville, NC

Preface

This book is written from the heart of a mother. I hope it will be a blessing to all mothers and individuals who have at some time in their lives faced tragedy. The content of these pages is very real and factual. There were so many times we felt we had lost the long, hard battle of recuperation, but we reached up and God took hold of our hands and He held on tightly. He never let us go. Praise His name!

Isaiah 43:2 reminds us that "When thou passeth through the waters, I will be with thee; and through the rivers, they shall not overflow thee: when thou walkest through the fire, thou shalt not be burned; neither shall the flame kindle upon thee. *Nahum 1:7* states, "The Lord is good, a strong hold in the day of trouble; and He knoweth them that trust in Him." *Indeed!*

The awesome power of prayer is demonstrated over and over again. Our Heavenly Father is magnified. His awesome power, mercy and grace were evident with every step of our journey. *Hebrews 4:15–16* affirms: "For we have not an high priest which cannot be touched with the feeling of our infirmities; but was in all points tempted like as we are, yet without sin. Let us therefore come boldly unto the throne of grace, that we may obtain mercy, and find grace to help in time of need."

God has a plan for every one of our lives. He knows what will happen before it comes to pass. He is the best friend we will ever have; and no matter how deep our individual valleys are or how high the mountains appear, Christ will never leave or forsake us. And he is always right on time. As we're lovingly reminded in *Luke 12:6–7*: "Are not five sparrows sold for two farthings, and not one of them is forgotten before God? But even the very hairs of your head all are numbered. Fear not therefore: ye are of more value than many sparrows."

I could not have written this book without God's inspiration. *Luke 11:9* promises, "Ask and it shall be given unto you; see, and you shall find; knock, and it shall be opened unto you." *Psalm 50:15b* claims that "I will deliver thee, and though shall glorify me." My desire is for the Lord to receive all the glory!

I also desire that by reading this book that you will remember daily (hourly!) to treasure your children (*Psalm 127:3* declares that, "Lo, children are an heritage of the Lord and the fruit of the womb is his reward."). Also treasure your spouse, your parents, your family, your friends—*all* those you value. Remember to hold them near and dear not only in your heart, but also in your arms: *Demonstrate* your love for them. Don't take them for granted. They can be gone in a blink of an eye. *Today, tell and show those individuals how special and priceless they are.*

Table of Contents

Introduction

My name is Margaret Harrison. My son Preston was in an automobile accident on Tuesday, September 9, 1997. This book is an account of our tragedy, our struggles, and how God gave us strength as a family to survive. It is dedicated to friends and family who helped us, and to my Aunt Margaret who died with cancer exactly two years (September 9, 1995) before Preston's accident. She was my role model and inspiration.

There are many support groups for families and victims who have had traumatic brain injuries. Please note the resource appendix. I encourage anyone who has experienced such an injury to seek help—help *is* available.

God has not promised
Skies always blue,
Flower-strewn pathways
All our lives through.
God has not promised
Sun without rain,
Day without sorrow,
Peace without pain.

But God has promised
Strength for today,
Rest for the labor,
Light for the way,
Grace for the trials,
Help from above,
Unfailing sympathy,
Undying love…

Chapter 1
Bad News Arrives

Tuesday, September 9, 1997: It was a beautiful fall afternoon. Over the last month, I was recovering from surgery and had been at home with my boys. The week before, we had revival at our church, Peace Haven Baptist, and had attended a youth rally on Saturday night. We were all tired and looked forward to being at home together.

The night before, my son Preston and I had our nightly devotions. We also had a good "mother-son" talk. I valued these precious times.

The next morning when Preston left for school, I said, "I love you, and drive carefully!" Preston was 16 years old and had just got his driver's license in June. He had driven with us for one year, and we knew he was a responsible driver, but mothers always dispense caution.

That evening I had planned a nice, quiet dinner for us that included Preston's favorite foods. Around three o'clock, the phone rang. The guidance counselor at school was calling to tell me bad news. He told me to stay calm: Preston had been in an accident, and his condition was critical. He was being transported to North Carolina Baptist Hospital in Winston-Salem.

Baptist Hospital has one of the best trauma centers in our area, and individuals in need of dire medical attention are usually transported there. I knew the situation must be grave. I immediately called my mother, who not only lives beside us but who's also my best friend, and relayed the news.

My brother was off from work that day, and he drove us to the hospital. It was no accident that my brother was home that day—I felt God had it all in His plan! Before we left home I called our preacher Bruce Freeman and left a plea on his answering machine for intercessory prayer for our son.

On the day of the accident, it had rained and the roads were wet and slippery. Preston had swerved his car to avoid a car that was turning across the road in front of him. This movement caused his car to hydroplane, hit a culvert and flip. The impact ejected Preston 20 feet in the air from the car. God's loving hand protected Preston by letting him land in a soft, wet tobacco field instead of the hard pavement. The car landed on its side. If it had flipped one more time, it would have crushed him. It's as if angels just held it to keep it from falling on Preston.

I didn't know that the helicopter from Baptist Hospital wasn't flying that day because of foul weather conditions. An ambulance had picked up Preston at the accident; he was so critical that the paramedics stopped at a local hospital, Hoots Memorial Hospital in Yadkinville, to stabilize him. If they hadn't stabilized him, permanent brain damage or even death was a real possibility.

The accident resulted in a major head injury and internal bleeding. He was having seizures, and the doctors had to insert a breathing tube in his throat. It was

extremely important to maintain oxygen flow to the brain to prevent permanent brain damage. One of the students who witnessed the accident said she was amazed Preston had even survived.

My sister and aunt were at Hoots Hospital when the doctors were trying to stabilize Preston. A nurse told them that Preston's eyes had already begun to set as the ambulance was leaving for Baptist Hospital. This is often an indication of a lack of brain activity!

The guidance counselor tried to reach us again, but we had already left for Baptist Hospital. Actually, it was good that I didn't go to Hoots Hospital because I would have "lost it." I was already very stressed, not knowing the extent of his injuries.

I waited about two hours at Baptist Hospital with

my mother and brother before Preston arrived in the ambulance. A brother-in-law, Kim, arrived shortly after we arrived at the hospital. He had already been by Hoots Memorial to check on Preston and knew that the situation was critical. Therefore, he wouldn't divulge the entire details of Preston's condition.

I called my sister who works at Hoots Memorial where the stabilization was in progress to ask her about Preston's condition, but she couldn't tell me the entire news. I knew something was terribly wrong! I thought, *What if Preston dies, and I'm not with him?*

Preston was saved at the age of 11, but I just couldn't give him up. Children remain our babies regardless of their age. I cried out to God to be with Preston! Our youth pastor, a devout soldier for Christ, also came to be with us and I needed this sense of security.

My husband David, who works at R.J. Reynolds Tobacco Company, was out in the plant and couldn't be found immediately. After finally getting the message, he arrived at the trauma center about 10 minutes before Preston arrived. I was so thankful to have my Christian husband with me.

You notice I said my Christian husband. David and I had been married for 20 years and he had just given his life to Christ five years earlier. God directs us in *II Corinthians 6:14*, "Be ye not unequally yoked together with unbelievers." We went through much turmoil during the first 15 years of our marriage. Many times I would cry out to God and ask, *Why does it have to be this way?*

Many times I considered separation, but the Holy Spirit would not let me do it! Preston grew up for 11 years in this situation and he was the one who finally convinced his father to go to church with us. What a difference it made when my husband got saved! We had fewer arguments and much less marital strain. It was like being married to a new man.

I could have saved Preston and myself a lot of grief if I had listened to the Holy Spirit when David and I got married, but love is blinding. Thank goodness that my

husband and I were both devoted Christians before this trial: I knew we were facing a very emotional period following this accident, and we needed God now more than ever to keep things together and guide us.

Thoughts of a Young Father

God has entrusted to me, a son.
I have prepared so little to give
In return. Yet, I must take him by
The hand and start him on his way.

I must teach him right from wrong,
When I am only half through my days,
Still searching for the truth.

I must hold tight, but not too tight.
I must hold long, but not too long.
I must lead him straight so he may
Choose his road. He will know love,
For mine will be with him, forever.

Then I must release him.
And watch him go alone, as he
Walks the road of life. Before he
Knows the weight his legs must carry.

Oh God, stay with him.

I know the pitfalls and lost labors
Sorrowed. Give him the comfort I had
When I, alone with You, walked that road.

—John Wescott

Chapter 2
A Long Night Ahead

Preston finally arrived at the trauma center at Baptist Hospital. I cannot describe the feeling inside when I saw my son at death's door. He had a breathing tube in his throat and intravenous lines for fluids and blood. He was unresponsive. I had been a nurse for 20 years, but now all my nursing knowledge seemed useless! My role now was that of a mother—my family was receiving medical help, not administering it.

A social worker was with us as Preston arrived. One of the security guards said that we should stay back from the ambulance. They didn't realize how badly we needed even just one glimpse of our son to get us through our fear. The social worker told them to let us see Preston.

We didn't interfere with the care Preston was receiving. My husband cried out to him, "Hold on, be strong!" even though Preston couldn't hear us.

We were then ushered to a small family consultation room to wait for an update. I had worked at Baptist Hospital for many years. I had been to a similar room like this when my father died. *Was I about to lose my son?*

The attending emergency room doctor was an emergency medicine specialist. He was very frank with us. He didn't give us any hope for Preston to survive. Preston had three immediate problems: The first was a closed head injury with increased swelling. The second was internal bleeding. The last and least critical was a laceration on his knee that needed sutures. I appreciated the doctor's honesty with us. We felt helpless, but we knew God truly was the Great Physician! Even if these earthly doctors saw little hope for Preston, God did.

Preston was immediately taken to surgery to correct the internal bleeding. Oh, how we needed God to intervene. Our faith was weak, but God was with us. The Bible tells us in *II Samuel 22:33*, "God is my strength and power." How directly and intensely we needed this verse.

Our pastor's wife had viewed the scene of the accident, and called her husband to the local hospital. He had followed the ambulance to Baptist Hospital. According to him, the ambulance made the trip in 11 crucial minutes. A local physician from Blue Ridge Cardiology had even accompanied Preston in the ambulance—a rare, divine occurrence.

Our pastor said that Preston was able to squeeze his hand on arrival to the emergency room at Yadkinville. After the paramedics delivered Preston to the care of the doctors, they began vigilant prayer! We're comforted in *II Corinthians 12:9–10* with, "My grace is sufficient for thee, for my strength is made perfect in weakness. For when I am weak, then am I strong."

This gave us encouragement! You see, Preston was called to be a preacher at 12 years of age. We hoped that God was not finished with Preston yet!

We remained in the surgery waiting room while

Preston was in surgery. It was amazing how many friends and members of our church family came to comfort us. The waiting room was full in a matter of hours. We never knew how much our church family meant to us until we faced this crisis.

For two long hours—120 minutes that felt like an eternity—we waited. Finally the doctor reported that Preston had survived the surgery. The source of bleeding was a ruptured spleen, which they had removed. He told us the next 48 hours would be crucial and warned us the road ahead would not be an easy one. We were also told that Preston had to be brought out of shock as soon as possible. The treatment for shock was to give fluids and blood. If he was given too much fluid, it would cause the pressure to increase in his head. With the closed head injury, this would be a "touch-and-go" situation. We had to take it hour by hour.

At 11 p.m. we got to see Preston and hold his hand. I just needed to touch my son, and what a joy it was to touch him. He had a screw in his head to measure the pressures. The goal was to keep the pressure reading at less than 20 and it was now holding around 14. *So far, so good!*

The skull does not "give," and when swelling occurs, the brain inside is simply damaged. No operation relieves this swelling. Preston had been prescribed medications to keep him "paralyzed," and this would assist in keeping his pressures down. We were assured that this was temporary. He had tubes and monitors everywhere. His

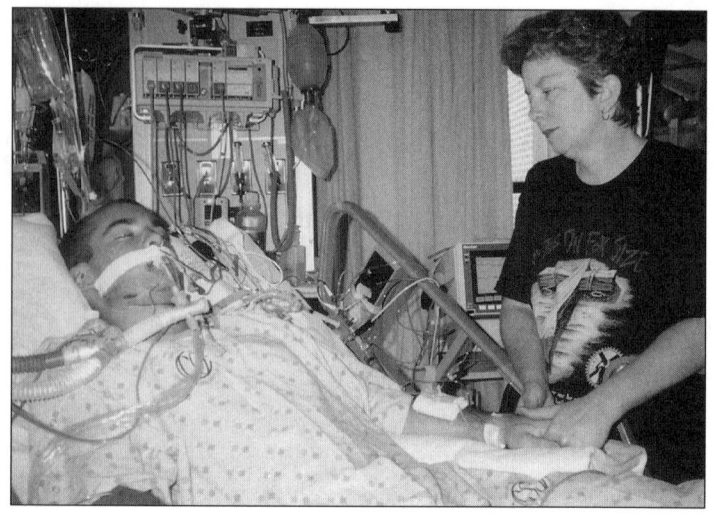

face and arms were so swollen. It was overwhelming and heart wrenching.

He also had two new problems that were not identified before surgery. When he was thrown from the car, his heart had been bruised, resulting in a very irregular heart rate that could cause his heart to stop at any time! He was given a medication called Lidocaine at a continuous rate. Preston also had a chest tube in his left side as a result of a collapsed lung. Many prayers were needed for him to survive.

This was the longest night of my life! But by the marvelous intervention of God between death and life, Preston made it through the night.

Making his rounds the next morning, the doctor warned there would be "bumps in the road," but this was to be expected. Those bumps turned out instead to be tall mountains. He anticipated various infections, and it would take two or three days to get him out of shock. That morning Preston received two more units of blood, which helped the shock condition, plus it provided extra oxygen to his brain. The blood had to be injected slowly to prevent an increase in cranial pressure.

On Wednesday night—the day after the accident— our family was supposed to meet with the Proteens group at our church. The other teens met, but no lesson was taught. They instead discussed the accident, vented their grief and prayed for Preston's condition. The Holy Spirit must have been present in a powerful and special way that evening. We could feel the prayers all the way to the hospital. My husband and I, along with friends and family, stayed in the lobby of the Intensive Care Unit. We managed to get a couple hours of sleep that night.

While Preston was at Baptist Hospital, we formed close friendships with several other people who had sick loved ones. We listened to each other, comforted each other, rejoiced together, and shed tears together. We still communicate with them and pray for them.

We could tell which families were Christians because they were able to cope with their tragedy a little better. Christ can help a person through anything. All things are possible to him who believes. In the Christian's life there's no substitute for Christ's presence to dispel the fear, panic and terror of the unknown. The families there who didn't have Christ were miserable and they struggled to be objective. We hoped our testimony could help them see how much they needed Christ. *Matthew 5:14, 16* says "Ye are the light of the world. Let your light shine before men, and glorify our father in heaven." In *Ephesians 5:8* we're directed to "walk as children of light."

We must uplift and magnify Christ in everything we do. As tragic as our situation was, others there had even more serious problems. All we had to do was look around.

There will always be something to do, my boy;
There will always be wrongs to right;
There will always be need for a manly breed,
And men unafraid to fight.

Thee will always be honor to guard, my boy;
There will always be hills to climb,
And tasks to do, and battles new
From now till the end of time.

There will always be dangers to face, my boy;
There will always be goals to take;
Man shall be tried, when the road divide,
And proved by the choice they make.

There will always be burdens to bear, my boy;
There will always be need to pray;
There will always be tears through the future years,
As loved ones are borne away.

There will always be God to serve, my boy,
And always the Flag above;
They shall call to you until life is through
For courage and strength and love.

So these are things that I dream, my boy,
And have dreamed since your life began:
That whatever befalls, when the old world calls,
It shall find you a sturdy man.

—Edgar A. Guest

Chapter 3
The Third Day

Preston survived the second night. At 11 a.m. we went into the ICU to see him. There were several nurses around him working diligently. We knew something was wrong!

The pressure on his brain was dangerously high and he was rushed to the X-ray department for another CAT scan. The hour's wait seemed endless. I know our children are only ours for a short time, but again I was so scared at the thought of giving him up now. Sixteen years with Preston just weren't enough.

When Preston was returned to ICU, a new medication called Mannitol was given to him supposedly to decrease the swelling. If the Mannitol didn't help, he would have to be induced into a deep coma. The nurses worked frantically to get this medication started. This was critical to prevent any permanent brain damage.

We called our church prayer chains, and they got through to heaven for us. *John 14:14* says, "If ye shall ask anything in my name, I will do it." Our friends got prayers started all over the United States from Pennsylvania to Texas. After about an hour, the medication began to help a bit and he was able to hold on through the night.

No Place for the Boys

What can a boy do, and where can a boy stay,
If he is always told to get out of the way?
He cannot sit here, and he must not stand there;
The cushions that cover the fine rocking chair
Were put there, of course, to be seen and admired;
A boy has no business to ever be tired.
The beautiful roses and flowers that bloom
On the floor of the darkened and delicate room
Are not made to walk on—at least not by boys;
The house is no place, anyway, for their noise.

Yet boys must walk somewhere; and what if their feet,
Sent out of our houses, sent into the street,
Should stop 'round the corner and pause at the door
Where other boys' feet have paused oft before;
Should pass through the gateway of glittering light,
Where jokes that are merry and songs that are bright
Ring a warm welcome with flattering voice,
And temptingly say, "Here's a place for the boys?"
Oh, what if they should! What if your boy or mine
Should cross o'er the threshold which marks out the line
"Twixt virtue and vice, "Twixt pureness and sin,
And leave all his innocent boyhood within?"

Oh what if they should, because you and I,
While the days and the months and the years hurry by,
Are too busy with cares and with life's fleeting joys

To make 'round our hearthstone a place for our boys!
There's a place for the boys. They'll find it somewhere;
And if our own homes are too daintily fair
For the touch of their fingers, the tread of their feet,
They'll find it, and find it, alas, in the street,
'Mid the guildings of sin and the glitter of vice.
And with heartaches and longings we pay a dear price
For the getting of gain that our lifetime employs,
If we fail to provide a good place for the boys.

—author unknown

There was something significant about the third day. Christ arose on the third day, and we prayed that Preston would, too! The medication was helping to a degree, and again Preston held on through another night.

Chapter 4
The Long Days Ahead

On Friday, September 12, Preston's temperature sky-rocketed again. It was dangerously high, and pneumonia had set in. The staff did a broncoscopy and administered antibiotics. The doctors said he had aspirated while he was having seizures. This condition was a result of the severe blow to his head. Aspiration occurs when vomit is swallowed into the lungs. After about 24 hours, we could see a degree of improvement.

On Saturday, the paralytic drugs were stopped. We hoped so much he would wake up, but there was still no response. He remained in a coma as his fever climbed to 103°. We begged God to have mercy on Preston and touch him with His healing powers.

We showered at the hospital and a family member was always in the waiting room in case we were needed. We slept in chairs or on the floor each night, which gave us no real rest, just an accumulated sense of sleep deprivation.

Some of our friends we'd met in the ICU waiting room saw improvement in the status of their loved ones, but it was depressing that Preston had no change from his comatose condition. While happy for our friends, we were hurting badly inside. We were hoping God was saving the best for last.

Some of these friends lost their loved ones. We weren't

sure what to say, but God supplied the words; it was comforting for us just to be there with them and listen as they expressed their grief. Strangely, it made us feel a little guilty that we still had our son.

Love is the treasure that multiplies by division.
It is the one gift that grows bigger the more you
take from it. It is the one business in which it pays
to be an absolute spendthrift. You can give it away,
throw it away, empty your pockets, shake the basket,
turn the glass upside down, and tomorrow you
will have more than ever!

—Author Unknown

Chapter 5
Things Are Looking Up

We put headphones to Preston's ears in hopes that he could hear them even though he couldn't respond. Hearing is the last sense that is lost. We also talked to him, hoping he would awaken at any minute. One of his friends read to him from the Bible. His heart rate actually slowed down as if he heard it! It seemed to relax him.

We began to see involuntary responses from Preston like the blinking of his eyes, a cough when his breathing tube was suctioned, and a slight clinching of his hands. But still he couldn't respond to commands. *John 15:16* says, "Ye have not chosen me, but I have chosen you, and ordained you, that ye should go and bring forth fruit and that your fruit should remain: that whatsoever ye shall ask of the Father in my name, he may give it to you." We were thankful for these incremental changes, and we were clinging to every moment and anticipating even greater changes.

By this time my husband David had gone back to work on second shift. I remained at the hospital. After his shift, David would come back to the hospital, and we would sleep in the lobby. The summer before Preston's wreck, we had gone on a mission trip to Jamaica. With none of the conveniences of home, we learned to be flexible in regard to where we slept. We employed this

Preston holds one of the friends he made during a mission trip to Jamaica the year before his accident.

talent well during the weeks ahead.

A family member would usually stay with us overnight. The comfort from our family and friends was indeed a rich blessing.

My mother was keeping our younger son Patrick who was then 10 years old—comforting him and getting him to and from school daily. Each afternoon she and Patrick quickly prepared his lessons for the next day, and then they came to visit Preston. Each day Mother and Patrick expected to find Preston awake, but it simply wasn't yet time for him to open his little chinquapin eyes and grin at them. Patrick was very disappointed that Preston wasn't making a connection with him.

One night the nurse woke me and my brother around midnight. Preston was again showing some signs of increased pressure in his head. They had to do another emergency CAT scan to determine if any fluid had accumulated. When my husband arrived at 1 a.m. we were sitting in the hall praying.

Immediately my husband called our pastor to let him know the problem. He got on his knees as soon as they got off the phone. By 3 a.m., Preston's condition had improved. What power prayers have! It was good to have a pastor to call on when we needed his fervent prayers. What agonizing hours a pastor goes through for his "flock of sheep."

The situation reminds me of a song that says: "Telephone to glory; Oh, what joy divine, I can feel the current moving on the line. Built by God the Father for His loved and own; we may talk to Jesus through the Royal Telephone."

The numeral nine has significance: it signifies finality or judgment. Nine is also three times three, signifying divine completeness. By the ninth day following the accident, we were completely exhausted.

We hadn't slept in a real bed since the wreck. A social worker offered us a room at the Ronald McDonald House near the hospital. We accepted her offer because Preston was relatively stable.

Our younger son Patrick often came with his grandmother at night to see us at the hospital. He loved his brother, and the ordeal had a great impact on him. My heart ached terribly to be with both my boys.

Patrick's grades started to drop, and he

Preston and his baby brother, Patrick.

was having a hard time coping. When he went home each night, he would cry to stay with us. We knew he needed our focus and attention also. We strived to include him in everything that involved Preston's condition.

On weekends, Patrick stayed with us at the Ronald McDonald House. Thank goodness for that place—it was a home away from home. Many new friendships were made there also. We comforted each other, one day at a time. We ended up staying there 40 nights. There is significance in the 40 nights—Moses was on the mountain for 40 days with God. Also Noah and his family endured the flood for 40 days and nights. The numeral 40 signifies a trial; it is the period of full probation, of complete testing.

As our days of testing continued, Preston was slowly weaned from the ventilator that was breathing for him. At first, he was too weak to breathe on his own, but finally he began to gain strength. A trach had been placed in his throat to prevent damage to his vocal cords. This device was a small airway inserted below his Adam's apple to convey air into the windpipe. He would have to learn to breathe all over again.

With brain injuries patients have what they call "hypothalamic storms." If a person gets easily excited, the heart rate goes up, along with the blood pressure, to a dangerously high level. Because of the location of the brain injury, Preston started having these hypothalamic storms and his body's "thermostat" had been damaged. He had episodes when his temperature would increase without any infection present at all. It would elevate to a dangerously high 103–104°.

To reduce his temperature, a cooling blanket was placed beneath him with a fan blowing directly on him at the same time. His body shivered violently. My heart was crushed at the sight. I wanted to wrap him in a good, warm blanket and hold him in my arms as I did when he was a baby; however, I realized that this course of action was necessary. We were in for an education—medically, emotionally and spiritually!

I wanted to take away my child's pain. I wanted to be near him, help him. Sometimes I truly thought Preston could hear me when I would whisper "Mama's here" and tell him where he was. Sometimes it would even calm his heart rate a little. It has been proven that touch can relax and calm a fast heart rate.

Preston was still comatose, but he was starting to have yawns. His neurosurgeon said this was a positive sign. We were excited! Preston's pediatrician began visiting about once a week. We were grateful to have an old friend who was like part of our family. We were elated over the slight improvements, but scared even to think about getting to a "mountaintop" because we knew how badly it hurt to fall back down. Yet God was always there to comfort us through every step of the journey.

The medications that Preston were given for the hypothalamic storms did not help. (We were not allowed to talk to Preston or touch him during this time.) Another medication called Thorazine was initiated and this acted directly at the injury location, but it produced a negative side effect: It's addictive. Nobody told us, and this was probably best. Finally, the Thorazine began to work.

At this point we had been in the ICU for two weeks. Preston was turned every two hours to prevent skin breakdown. We certainly didn't want him to get bedsores on top of everything else. He had no control of his bowels or bladder, and he had to wear a diaper. We had to keep his skin as dry as possible. The nurse got him in a recliner at times for a change of position. At last he was taken off the ventilator and moved to the Pediatric Intensive Care Unit (PICU).

A Boy's Prayer

Dear God, if You could spare the time
To let my dog lie down beside Your feet.
Or send an angel to the gate to meet
Him when he comes, I would be glad;
For we have never been apart until today,
And, even in Heaven, I know he will be sad.
And, please appoint a friendly boy angel—
One who has no doggy ghost to call his own—
Who occasionally will pat my pup
And offer him a choice celestial bone.
I would not grieve so if I knew
My dog had found a home with You!

—Mary Ellen Stelling

Chapter 6
A Whole New Ball Game

Preston was 16 years old—still an adolescent. He was so sick when he was admitted to the hospital that no one realized his age. He was initially taken to the adult trauma unit at Baptist Hospital; then they realized his age. When he was moved to PICU, we were able to visit him more. We were told that the family should be involved with the patient's care as much as possible. Family interaction with the patient speeds up recovery time.

Preston continued to have the increased temperature and hypothalamic storms. It was difficult to understand why things had to get worse before they got better.

Every night I read from my Bible and cried myself to sleep. It is untold how many tears my husband and I shed for our son. Daily we had to learn how to pray and trust God completely. We knew we had to give Preston to the Lord and let His will be done—whatever God's will was.

Every night my eyes would turn to *Psalm 136*. This psalm expresses how God's mercy and grace endureth forever. My husband David kept reading *Job*. His favorite passage was *Job 2:6*: "And the Lord said unto Satan, Behold, he is in thine hand; but save his life." David never got mad at God. We always thanked Him and praised Him for what He had already done for us—our son was still alive.

God continued to provide good doctors and nurses who knew where their wisdom originated. God was working through them and continued to provide for our needs. *I Thessalonians 1:3* reminds us, "Remembering without ceasing your work of faith, and labor of love, and patience of hope in our Lord Jesus Christ." When we face trials, His strength becomes greater in our weakness. When we turn it all over to Him, "the power of Christ" rests upon us. We do not face trials because we are being punished. Remembering that God knows the end from the beginning, our suffering is eased and the pain made bearable.

Trials would be easier to bear if we could remember that by enduring something that we may regard as a hindrance or handicap, we can bring more glory to God than if that undesired thing was removed. The glorious fact is that these don't have to be born in our own feeble strength, but by His power in us!

The bills continued to accumulate, and I was unable to work. In our hearts, my husband and I decided that Preston needed me most, even though this brought no paycheck. My friends at work donated their vacation hours for us. I was blessed to receive a month's pay without even asking. At my husband's workplace, people collected money for us. The car Preston wrecked was obviously a total loss. The insurance adjuster came by and paid what the car was worth, allowing us to pay the loan balance. This was one less debt to worry about. God always knows how to give us a ray of sunlight when we need it.

God was good to us in many ways. He sent people to talk with us whom we didn't know. Some of these people had had similar tragedies and their children were now doing well. It seemed that God always sent words of encouragement to us at when we needed them most.

We met a family from our community whose daughter had also been in a serious automobile accident. We'd seen them at ball games, but never really knew them. Their daughter also had a closed head injury, but it was not as serious as Preston's. Her parents "camped out" near us in the same corner of the Intensive Care Unit.

Bless the Lord, O my soul; and
All that is within me, bless his holy name.
Bless the Lord, O my soul; and
Forget not all his benefits.
Who forgiveth all think iniquities;
Who healeth all thy diseases;
Who redeemeth thy life from
Destruction; who crowneth thee
With loving-kindness and tender
Mercies.
The Lord is merciful and gracious,
Slow to anger, and plenteous
In mercy.
He hath not dealt with us after
Our sins; nor rewarded us according
To our iniquities.
Like as a father pitieth his children,
So the Lord pitieth them that fear him.
Bless the Lord, all his works in
All places of his dominion; bless the
Lord, O my soul.

Psalm 103: 1-4, 8, 10, 13, 22

Chapter 7
Who Cares?

We arrived at the hospital early one morning. Preston's temperature was 105° and his heart rate exceeded 200 beats per minute! He was posturing severely as if he was having a horrible seizure.

Preston's nurse was writing notes on another patient, and she appeared cavalier about the situation. It was a big deal to me, and as Preston's mother, I did not handle the situation objectively! We had requested that we be called if there was any change in Preston's condition. No one had called us. Parents have a right to be advocates for their sick children. This was my new full-time job—being Preston's advocate until he could speak for himself.

Preston had developed an infection in his blood from one of the intravenous lines. We immediately called to begin the prayer chain. We could feel the prayers, especially those of our widows who are mighty prayer warriors in our church. Our widows are especially faithful! *Hebrews 4:16* says "Let us therefore come boldly unto the throne of grace, that we may obtain mercy and find grace to help in time of need."

Our doctor worked long hours so we hardly saw him. On the weekends, he wasn't around. It always seemed as though Preston had problems on Saturday or Sunday and we needed his primary doctor.

I knew the doctor couldn't work around the clock, but I wished he could. He always listened to us, even if there was nothing he could do. In hindsight, perhaps the staff wasn't optimistic about Preston's recovery.

In the Bible it tells us that if we have faith as small as a mustard seed, God will move mountains. During this time, I felt my faith was indeed this tiny, and I was weak. Yet I knew that through the years God had always provided for our needs according to His riches in glory.

As I left Preston's side, with my eyes filled with tears, I turned to see a complete stranger that God had sent to minister to me. A lady I'd never met came to see us that very night. Her son had also been in a severe automobile accident and was in the hospital for an extended time with even more complications than Preston. Her son went to a rehabilitation center in Charlotte for several weeks after being discharged from Baptist. I thought, *Oh, no, what else will we have to do after we leave here?* Charlotte seemed so far away from home and family. (Brenner Children's Hospital is currently building a rehabilitation facility, but to date Charlotte provides the closest center that works with children and adults.)

The lady shared more scripture to help comfort us. She read *Mark 11:22–24*: "And Jesus answering saith unto them, Have faith in God. For verily I say unto you that whosoever shall say unto this mountain, be though removed, and be thou cast into the sea; and shall not doubt in his heart, but shall believe that those things which he saith shall come to pass; he shall have whatsoever he saith. Therefore I say unto you, what things soever ye desire when ye pray, believe that ye receive them, and ye shall have them." Praise God! He knew that we needed this encouragement and hope at that exact moment!

As the infection in Preston's blood improved, a gastrostomy tube or feeding tube was inserted into his stomach. We were told that Preston needed this because he had a long period of recovery ahead of him. This tube would also prevent irritation of the sinuses, which could cause more complications. Preston had lost 30 pounds since his accident: He had dropped from 136 pounds to 106 pounds at this point.

The insertion of a gastrostomy tube is usually a simple procedure. However, the doctor explained that they had to do a surgical procedure to insert the tube. Preston's stomach had floated under the ribs into the space his spleen had once occupied.

Preston continued to receive the strong antibiotic Vancomycin because he continued to have temperature elevations. He did yawn more, but that was the only positive response he had. Our family reached for and firmly grasped every thread of hope.

His temperature fluctuated and climbed. A new team of doctors was called who dealt with infectious diseases. Preston's blood work showed an elevation of his white count to 23,000, indicating an infection. The normal white count is 5,000–10,000. A new antibiotic was started and seemed to help temporarily.

Preston's heart rate became more irregular and a

cardiologist was consulted. The doctors treated the irregularity with medication, but it seemed to be coming solely from the pressure associated with the closed head injury. I was a mama now, but my nursing background made me uneasy and troubled. My husband and I sensed there was more to it than what the doctors divulged.

Beauty

The sunshine was gentle
On his little blond head,
As he bent over something
And gleefully said,

"Mommy, come look
See what I've found.
A beautiful something's
Come up from the ground."

Before I could reach him,
He was holding up high
Our first purple crocus;
I wanted to cry.

But, I could remember
When beauty had said
To me, too, "Come touch"
So I hugged him instead.

—Brenda K. Graham

Chapter 8
A New Challenge

Twenty-two days after the accident, Preston was still in the ICU. Even though Preston was still in a coma, the doctors felt rehabilitation therapy should be started. When muscles are inactive for a prolonged period, they forget what to do. Even though he was asleep, his muscles needed conditioning. This need for rehabilitation somehow made us feel as if a ray of sunlight had broken through the clouds and surely there was hope for our precious son. Little did we know what a hard road lay before us.

The first therapist we met was an occupational therapist. She worked with his arms and hands and tried to stimulate Preston to wake up. As she exercised his arms, she demonstrated what we could do when she wasn't around. The therapist made splints for his hands to prevent contractures. The splints were worn two hours on and two off. We brought pictures of family and friends to hang above his bed so when he woke up, it might trigger his memory. The therapist was very patient with Preston even though no response surfaced for some time.

Our second therapist was a physical therapist. She dealt with the muscles in his legs and feet. His feet muscles and ligaments had weakened and lost all muscle tone; they had atrophied to the extent that he would never be able to walk with them in this condition. She started a series of putting new casts on his feet every week. Incrementally his feet were pushed closer to a 90° bend.

Since the rehabilitation therapy had started, Preston was beginning to have pain in his legs even though he was still in a coma. The new exercises had stimulated some involuntary movements. We knew he was having cramps in his legs because we could feel the muscles tighten. This problem was added to the "storms" that he continued to have.

His neurosurgeon told us the swelling had decreased in Preston's head for now, and he was going to stop the seizure medication.

These were all good signs. I didn't know how to act on this mountain top. All I could do was cry and thank and praise God for watching over us! It was refreshing to hear good news.

Twenty-five days after the wreck Preston stretched and yawned as if he might wake up. It looked so natural! Oh, what a disappointment when he didn't wake up. His heart rate was still erratic and climbing, but his "posturing" activity was improving.

A schoolmate of Preston's visited this day. He had been in an automobile accident a year ago and was in a coma for 12 days. His stay in the hospital and rehabilitation center was three months total. There was no outward sign he had ever been in such a traumatic accident. He looked great! He gave me such hope for Preston's future. Could our son ever look like him?

The following day a housemother from the Ronald McDonald House told us about her son who was also in a similar accident. She said he had married and has a family now. That sounded like a distant dream to us at this point. It was good encouragement to us. God knew we needed it!

The occupational therapist came in the next day. She had been flipping her fingers at Preston's eyelashes to see if he would blink. So far there had been no response, but this day he did blink. She said this was a positive sign. We were elated!

Preston's white count had come down to 15,000 and they were going to move him from the ICU to a regular hospital floor.

> *Although the threads of my life*
> *Have often seemed knotted, I know*
> *By faith, that on the other side*
> *Of the embroidery there is a crown.*

> —Corrie Ten Boom

Chapter 9
What a Relief

We were moved to the adolescent unit, room 747. I remember it because of the jet of the same name. What a difference in this new environment. It was a less stressful atmosphere and quieter without all the monitors and beeping noises. We had heard these for 27 days. I didn't realize what a jarring, restless effect those constant noises could have on the body and mind.

Now we actually had peace and quiet. I could stay with my son all the time and take care of him. In the ICU, we had to limit visitation; it was their policy, plus Preston was usually unstable. We still had to limit visitors because his resistance was low. I also didn't want others to see him looking like this. I recalled *Romans 8:28*, which proclaims "And we know that all things work together for good to them that love God, to them who are called according to His purpose."

Our family helped us tremendously through these weeks. My mother-in-law stayed with Preston in the mornings so I could nap. I was so appreciative of this small daily break. Because of the constant attention Preston required from the nurses, none of us got much rest at night.

As a parent, you also hear every move your children make when they're sick. Sitting by Preston in his hospital bed were quiet times I had alone with God. I would always pray with Preston even though I wasn't sure he could hear me. I read a scripture verse each day to him.

My husband also gave me strength. He would call from work several times a night to check on us. Late in the evening, both our brothers would visit. It was such a sacrifice for them to work each day and then visit almost every day. We were thankful for everyone's support.

Every day after school, Mother would bring my Patrick to see Preston. They would stay as long as they could. If Patrick had any homework he hadn't finished, I would help him. This emotional ordeal had made such an impact on Patrick. He couldn't concentrate on school-work with Preston in such a condition. He almost failed the fourth grade during this trial.

On Fridays, I would allow family members to stay with Preston so I could get a solid night's sleep. David, Patrick and I would stay together at the Ronald McDonald House. Patrick needed this attentive love and special time. On Monday nights, the Ronald McDonald House provided McDonald's food, and Patrick especially looked forward to this particular treat.

On Thursday night, the Ronald McDonald House had bingo. Patrick enjoyed playing bingo. The first night we went, I had a hard time coping with it. Two teen-aged boys from a local school donated their time. They were about Preston's age, and deep inside I was aching because I wanted Preston to wake up and be his old self again. These boys reminded me so much of him. I thought, *I don't have the courage to go back there again*, and yet God renewed my strength and gave me that courage! We must face our problems head on. We cannot avoid what hurts us.

Now that Preston was on a regular floor, we could turn on the television and let Preston listen to games or other familiar programs. We were hoping familiar sounds might rouse him. We continued talking to Preston, keeping him informed about his surroundings and all the things he was missing. He received many flowers that he never saw, but we told him about each arrangement.

Every day we walked through one experience after another. His hair had grown and not been cut in 28 days. Preston always took great pride in how he looked, so I was determined to help him! He liked his hair short. I brought my clippers and my mother-in-law helped me hold his head so I could cut his hair. Oh, how handsome he looked! We all also got an education in how to shave another person—it was quite an experience.

The next day, the physical therapist brought an assistant to support Preston's back and head and sat him on the side of the bed. What a wonderful sight it was to see my son sitting again, even though it wasn't with his own strength. It was progress nonetheless.

We had been told about the rehabilitation center in Charlotte and wanted to go there badly. This center had techniques to stimulate Preston to wake up that Baptist Hospital just didn't have.

One night after everyone else had left, I was alone with Preston. It was about 9 p.m., and Preston's neurosurgeon came to check on him. The neurosurgeon suggested that we put Preston in a skilled nursing home. I refused. We wouldn't send Preston to a nursing home—we would take him home first and attempt to take care of him until he no longer needed us. We were determined to give him all the strength and vigor we had. *How could the doctor ask us such a question?* I was disappointed in the doctor, but his question served to buoy my faith to a higher level. I would not give up on my son. With God's help, we would continue this climb, this journey, to bring my son back.

God
Is the master builder.
His plans are perfect and true.
And when He sends you sorrow,
It's part of His plan for you.
For all things work together
To complete the master plan,
And God up in His heaven
Can see what's best
For man.

A few hours later, a friend called and said that they were still praying for Preston. She said he was on a prayer chain in Texas. There is mighty power in prayer! *James 5:16* tells us that "The effective fervent prayer of a righteous man availeth much." God knew I needed this encouragement and God is always right on time. Little did my friend know what I had just gone through, but God did.

Again, I was strengthened.

The next day, Preston's drafting teacher came to see him. The children in his vocational class had donated money for Preston. As the teacher talked to Preston, *his eyes amazingly opened*—such a simple yet profound act! He didn't respond, but what an awesome blessing it was to see him open his eyes after they were closed for so long! God knew we needed this miraculous boost after being confronted the night before with the unthinkable suggestion of putting Preston in a nursing home.

The book of *Psalms* tells us to "Be of good courage and He shall strengthen your heart, all ye that hope in the Lord." We asked our pastor to anoint Preston with oil. He came with deacons from our church, and they prayed and anointed Preston with oil. One of the deacons noted that Preston seemed particularly peaceful while they were praying over him. We believe that God is the Divine Healer and that He works through His chosen people. Doctors use the knowledge that God bestows upon them, and work through the inspiration of God.

We were praying things would quickly improve after Preston's eyes had opened. It was not in God's plan as Preston developed yet another complication. He got a bladder infection because his catheter had been inserted for so long and his white count was now 21,000. The Charlotte Rehabilitation Center would not accept him with this infection. This was another setback.

The proper exercise of patience is one of the difficulties of the spiritual life. If we do not see some immediate results, we're disappointed. For the soldier, marching is much easier than standing still. While it may seem an uneasy thing to wait on the Lord, it is one of the things a Christian soldier must learn to do, even if it takes years of training. God was still training us.

"There may have been long delays in the fulfillment of promises; but delays are not denials, and it is better to let the fruit ripen before you pluck it," said Dr. F. B. Meyer. *Psalm 37:7* tells us, "Rest in the Lord, and wait patiently for him: fret not thyself because of him who prospereth in his way, because of the man who bringeth wicked devices to pass."

A few more days passed, and Preston opened both eyes and raised his shoulders as if he were going to wake up. He even sneezed! In *Galatians 6:9* it says "And let us not be weary in well doing: for in due season we shall reap, if we faint not." We clung to these small yet marvelous happenings.

Most teens love soft drinks and Preston too had his favorite—Preston loved Mountain Dew. We put some Mountain Dew on a swab and put it in Preston's mouth hoping a favorite taste would stimulate him. He moved his lips as though he was tasting it, but it didn't wake him.

The next day his occupational therapist worked with him, and again his eyes were open. He followed pictures. He then got so excited that his heart rate increased to the point that she had to stop. He even responded when I spoke to calm him.

The medical staff did a CAT scan the next day. The

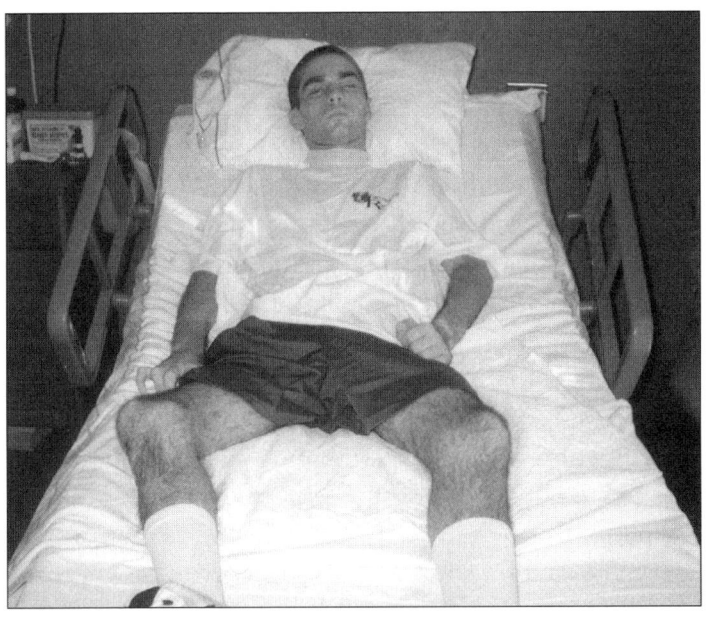

X-ray report showed some hydrocephalus, which is an accumulation of fluid on the brain. This condition requires surgery and the insertion of a drainage tube. What an awful discovery! Yet when the neurosurgeon reviewed the X-ray, he told us it was nothing to worry about. Again, we felt God's blessing.

It was now 39 days since the accident. We dressed Preston with a shirt and shorts. He looked so good and natural—much more like himself. We snapped a picture to capture this victory.

The physical therapist came later that day to sit him on the side of the bed. She put colored cones on his bed-side table. She asked him to pick a color, and he actually responded. What a miracle!

Before we could go to Charlotte, Preston had to be weaned off the addictive Thorazine. The doctors couldn't completely stop it immediately or Preston's body would go into shock with terrible withdrawal symptoms.

He continued to have painful cramps in his legs and arms and would cry out in extreme anguish even though he was not awake. Two people stayed with him around the clock. Preston's legs would knot up and tighten when they were cramping.

The only assistance I could offer was to massage his legs and apply heat, but nothing seemed to help. We begged the doctors for some kind of pain medication to help him through this suffering. They were reluctant to give him anything, but we insisted. We couldn't bear to see our son in such misery. It tore at our hearts each time he cried out.

Seeing my son in torment caused me immense grief. During his hospital stay I lost 15 pounds. Our family was enduring a real tribulation period, but *Romans 5:3–5* reminded us "but we glory in tribulations also: knowing that tribulation worketh patience; and patience, experience; and experience, hope: and hope maketh not ashamed; because the love of God is shed abroad in our hearts by the Holy Ghost which is given unto us." *Psalm 94:19* affirms: "When anxiety was great within me, your consolation brought joy to my soul."

There is never a day so dim
But God can make it bright.
And to the soul that seeks Him
He gives songs in the night.
There is never a path so hidden
But God can lead the way
If we seek for the Spirit's guidance
And patiently wait and pray.
There is never a cross so heavy
But Jesus' hands are there
To hold you with gentle compassion
The burden to help you bear.
There is never a heart so broken
But our loving Lord can heal
The heart that was pierced on Calvary
Does for his loved ones feel.
There is never a sin or sorrow
There is never a care or loss
But that we may bring to Jesus
And leave at the foot of the cross.

Chapter 10
A New Journey

We had been at Baptist Hospital for seven weeks. The number seven holds great significance in the Bible: Seven is the number of completion; it is the symbol of spiritual perfection. In *Ecclesiastes* we're told that "To every thing there is a season and a time to every purpose under heaven." This was the crucial time for the first stage of Preston's healing. This stage was only the beginning, and we didn't comprehend the valleys and mountains still awaiting us in this journey.

In light of his recent improvements, we were soon referred to the rehabilitation facility in Charlotte. We had to transfer Preston by ambulance, and our son Patrick rode in the front with the ambulance driver. Patrick's inclusion was always deliberate; we were determined to keep Patrick involved in his brother's life in every way possible. It was also our way of keeping our family more intact.

Our first day at the Charlotte Rehabilitation Center was an absolute nightmare! We met our new doctor who told us Preston would be started on a new muscle relaxant, but the pain medication would be stopped. She wanted him to wake up and proceed with his therapy. She appeared indifferent as to how much pain he was experiencing, but she assured us his distress would lessen.

This valley seemed to be one of the darkest. The

mental and physical stresses continued to wear on our family, but we clung to our hope that Preston would improve with this new care.

The doctor changed Preston's tracheostomy to a smaller size to help him learn to breathe without it. She did the procedure at his bedside. It took four of us to hold him down; he was in such pain. His shirt was so bloody afterward, we just cut it off. It was torture to watch my child endure this procedure.

That same night was just as horrendously stressful. My husband stayed with me, but we slept little. Every few minutes, Preston would cry out in agony. After midnight Preston was also catheterized for a urine sample in addition to what he had endured earlier that day. It was an exhausting, emotionally draining night. We eventually called my mother-in-law and aunt who came to relieve us. They were indeed a blessing to our weary bodies and battered hearts.

Similar to the Ronald McDonald House, Mae's Inn was a hospitality house located near the Charlotte facility for families to use at no cost. After a few hours of sleep at the inn, we hurried back to the hospital.

We soon met a psychologist who worked with a team of rehabilitation doctors. She specialized in the treatment of patients with head injuries. The Lord sent her to our family when we needed her expertise. The first question she asked us was, "How have you made it this far?" Our answer: "by God's grace." She had no response.

In *II Corinthians 12:9–10* it tells us that "My grace is

sufficient for thee: for my strength is made perfect in weakness. Most gladly therefore will I rather glory in my infirmities, that the power of Christ may rest upon me. Therefore I take pleasure in infirmities, in reproaches, in necessities, in persecutions, in distresses for Christ's sake: for when I am weak, then am I strong." The Harrisons were excessively weak at this point.

She explained to us how Preston's brain was damaged and how it would recover. This was exactly what we needed to hear—clear details. We had been in treatment for seven weeks, and no one had explained this in depth until now. It helped us to understand why Preston was acting the way he was.

It still didn't take away the pain, but it did help. She asked that we not respond to Preston when he would cry out; the stimulation was counterproductive. She encouraged us to keep the room quiet and dark—and it actually worked. She had warned he could use language he had never used before, but this never occurred. Thank goodness God prevented this additional insult to our struggle.

The next day, the occupational therapist came to dress Preston. This was part of the therapy to help him re-familiarize himself with routine activities. He was still comatose, but she started with his daily routine. Preston had gone from a vibrant, smart, 16-year-old to a two-year-old where his normal characteristics were concerned. He had forgotten how to eat, go to the bathroom and even dress himself. He had to wear a diaper and would need to be potty-trained again. His therapy would be intense: eight hours each day of physical, occupational and speech therapy. This would go from Monday to Friday and half a day on Saturday.

The new muscle relaxants were helping, but he still cried out in distress. He could be heard all the way down the hall. His patience was limited.

His trach was removed on the third day in Charlotte. On this memorable day we were able to lay him on a stretcher and give him a shower. This was his first shower in 50 days. He was shivering when he came back. His brain "thermostat" was still healing and its temperature regulation was problematic.

After the first week at the Charlotte facility, he was truly waking up and coming out the coma. *He was coming back to us.* Preston remembered the two most important things he could—his family and the fact he loved the Lord. *My son was back!* He didn't know why he was in the hospital. We told him of the accident and what the last few weeks had held. From this point on, Preston would remain out of the coma. We still had miles to go in crossing the mountain ranges, but now Preston would truly be aware of the journey.

The speech therapist began trying to teach Preston how to use his mouth muscles to eat. The therapist offered him some applesauce, but he didn't know what to do with it and didn't have the strength yet to eat.

Over the course of a week, Preston became more proficient in using his right side as opposed to his left.

His injury had impaired his entire left side. We noticed his hearing had been damaged on his left side—yet with his right ear he could hear minute noises of someone whispering across the room. His vision also suffered, and he needed a magnifying glass to read.

Between therapies, we would roll him in his wheelchair up and down the hall to keep him occupied. We soon learned where everything was in that hospital.

He began to write notes. The first note he wrote was "I love you." I still have that note. When I look at it, tears stream down my face because I realize, *What a miracle! What a miracle!*

Preston was soon able to arrange pegs in a pattern. He was so exhausted from long days of therapy that he was asleep each night at eight o'clock. It was all we could do to keep him awake until then.

During the day, he was not allowed to go back to bed on his lunch break. He wanted to lie down so badly. The therapist said it would help him get stronger if he stayed up. I couldn't resist letting my bone-weary son rest for a few minutes; my mother-in-law and I would find places to hide and let him prop his head on a pillow for a nap.

It was day number 51 since the wreck. Preston learned how to lick a lollipop. It was one of many momentous relearning occasions. On this day we rolled him outside where he could see the beautiful stream in front of the hospital. There was a paved sidewalk running beside it with easy access for wheelchairs.

The running water was calming for all of us and the

gentle sound was nature's therapy that we drastically needed. We picked up rocks and tried to skip them over the water. Preston thought it was funny and his laughter was a wonderful and glorious sound. He soon was able to throw small rocks himself. This was indeed a mountain-top day.

If in your heart you yearn to feel
A joy extremely rare,
Just gather up your worries and
Stroll in the country air.
Walk slowly down a shady lane,
Where songbirds harmonize,
Then let the wonder of the woods
Tenderly grace your eyes.
Reach out and touch the golden beams
That filter through the trees,
And fill your lungs with nature's bliss
That rides the incensed breeze.
Each step you take I guarantee,
Will make your troubles stray,
Dame Nature is a doctor that
Can drive all care away.
If you should tire, rest a while
Upon the moss-patched sod,
For you are close to heaven
In loving arms of God.

On post-accident day 52, October 30, the doctors gave us a discharge date of December 19, a seemingly eternity away. We decided to keep it a secret from Preston in case any problems arose.

We kept a calendar and marked off the days until Thanksgiving. What a joyous Thanksgiving we would have even if it was spent in the hospital. We had our son, and he was alive. It wouldn't be like home, but we would be together, which was the most important thing.

As therapy continued, Preston was able to stand on the parallel bars, and he was learning to swallow. He had advanced to eating soft foods. Friends sent some of his favorite desserts. We were glad of this progress because he needed to gain weight; he looked like a pile of bones.

On November 9, my husband and I went home for a night. My brother and his wife stayed with Preston at the hospital. Before we left, I told them our routines. I know I sounded like a new mother, but I couldn't help it. We left knowing he was in good hands.

This was the first time I had gone home since his accident. It was strange to see the outside world, and odd to be home without Preston. My, how wonderful our house looked after being away for so long. It felt like a mansion after being confined to lobbies and single rooms.

Preston was soon started on schoolwork, and he did better than we expected. Before the accident, he was an honor student. Now he was thinking on the level of a second grader. It was hard for us to adjust to this level, but we were simply thankful that we still had him.

We accepted him unconditionally. He was our son, just as he was. That is how Christ accepts us, just as we are. Once we are saved, God is always our Father, even when we mess up. In *Hebrews 13:5* we're told, "for he hath said, I will never leave thee, nor forsake thee." During our hospital stay, we saw children who never woke up. I can't comprehend what those families endured.

Preston continued to improve. He was soon able to handle a razor and shave. We would put the shaving cream on his face and hold his mirror. I was excited that

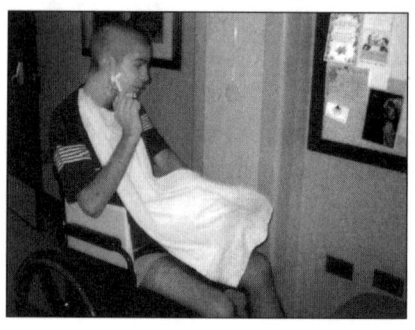

he could do it again—plus, it's a tough job to shave someone else.

Preston's resistance was now low from all his physical exertion, and he developed a head cold. My other son Patrick had developed strep throat, and Mother had taken him to the doctor for an antibiotic. It's funny how the prescription was filled: The pharmacist put it in two separate bottles. I naturally gave some of the medicine to Preston.

Finally Preston's feeding tube was removed. No anesthetic or sedation was used—the doctor just pulled it right out of his stomach. Frankly, he cursed. She said, "It didn't hurt too bad." He responded, "Yeah, it wasn't your stomach!" It was important to keep Preston on a high calorie diet. The problem was that he was too weak to eat very much.

Because of his lack of patience, which is typical of individuals who have suffered brain injuries, he was started on a drug called Ritalin—a drug used for children with Attention Deficit Disorder (ADD). Two side effects are nausea and stomach cramps. What bad timing! Preston's appetite decreased, and we were concerned that the feeding tube would have to be reinserted.

High calorie supplements were sent to him with his dinner meal. The dietician asked his favorite milkshake flavor, and we told her strawberry or vanilla. Naturally they would always send chocolate.

Our psychologist decided the Ritalin wasn't helping enough to risk a decreased appetite; therefore, it was discontinued and his appetite improved immediately.

He Leadeth Me

In pastures green? Not always; sometimes He
Who knoweth best, in kindness leadeth me
In many ways where heavy shadows be.
Out of the sunshine warm and soft and bright—
Out of the sunshine into the darkest night,
I oft would faint with sorrow and affright,
Only for this—I know He holds my hand;
So whether in the green or desert land
I trust although I may not understand.

And by still waters? No, not always so;
Ofttimes the heavy tempests round me blow,
And o'er my soul the waters and billows go.
But when the storms beat loudest and I cry
Aloud for help, the Master standeth by
And whispers to my soul, "Lo, it is I."
Above the tempest wild I hear Him say,
"Beyond this darkness lies a perfect day.
In every path of thine I lead the way."

So whether on the hilltops high and fair
I dwell, or in the sunless valleys where
The shadows lie—what matters? He is there.
So where He leads me, I can safely go,
And in the blest hereafter, I shall know
Why, in His wisdom, He hath led me so.

—Rev. John F. Chaplain

Chapter 11
A Sad Day

For four weeks the Charlotte hospital staff had allowed us to stay in Preston's room while he was undergoing therapy. Now his doctor decided that it was time for Preston to be on his own—day and night. I couldn't imagine leaving him during the day, much less leaving him there alone at night!

Baptist Hospital had encouraged family involvement. The Charlotte facility was now discouraging our involvement, and we wondered how we'd ever abide by their rules. *How could I leave my child?*

After receiving this news, I was in the hospital kitchen crying, and my mother-in-law was in Preston's room crying. Neither one of us knew what to say to each other. Just the thought of not being by Preston's side was hard for us to accept.

Because my husband David worked second shift, he normally came to Charlotte on Wednesdays to visit. This new regulation meant that my husband would get to see Preston only once each week. I knew when David heard about this he would be especially upset.

We tried to talk with the doctor, but it was her way or no way! We seriously thought of taking him home, but we knew he wasn't ready.

The Bible tells us in *James 1:19*, "My beloved brethren,

let every man be swift to hear, slow to speak, and slow to wrath." In *Ecclesiastes 7:9* it admonishes, "Be not hasty in thy spirit to be angry; for anger resteth in the bosom of fools." *Psalm 37:8* says, "Cease from anger, and forsake wrath; fret not thyself in any wise to do evil." We knew it wouldn't be good for Preston's well-being if we expressed anger and caused an unpleasant scene.

Because I was now only allowed to stay with Preston a limited amount of time during the day, I wanted to find a way he could reach me if he needed me. I wanted Preston to know it was not our choice to stay away. My husband brought our home phone to put in Preston's room. Preston's vision was impaired, and he couldn't see small letters or numbers. Our phone had large enough numbers for him to see. We programmed in the phone number to Mae's Inn so all he would have to do was to dial one button to reach me. With these new limited visitation restrictions I would stay at the inn until about three o'clock, then sneak back to Preston's room and wait on him until his therapy was done. After only the first day of this new schedule, I knew these next several days would be long ones.

He Giveth More Grace

He giveth more grace when the burdens grow greater,
He sendeth more strength when the labors increase;
To added affliction he addeth His Mercy
To multiplied trials, His multiplied peace.
His Love has no limit; His grace has no measure;
His power no boundary known unto men;
For out of His infinite riches in Jesus
He giveth and giveth and giveth again.

—Annie Johnson Flint

To help the time pass and to ease my dismay over not being able to stay with Preston, my brother came down one day and we went shopping. I've never been a shopper. I especially didn't know how to act now. I felt lost.

My brother- and sister-in-law came that same evening and my sister-in-law took me to the Southern Living Christmas Show in Charlotte. They had graciously pitched in to keep me busy, mentally and physically. I was thankful for their love and consideration, although my mind and heart stayed on my son.

Over the following slow-moving days, I worked on hobbies I liked such as cross-stitching and reading. I helped clean at the inn to stay busy. I would take advantage of the daylight and walk over to the hospital in the evenings; this was safe and good exercise. At night, I would ride the hospital van.

On Saturdays, my family would come to visit. My mother was allowed to stay on Saturday nights with Preston. David, Patrick and I would go to a local motel for the night because the inn wouldn't let children stay.

One weekend, some teens from our church came to visit Preston, and he enjoyed it so much. They brought him a ceramic eagle to look at for encouragement. The eagle was a symbol of strength that we used in our Proteens group studies. The verse that went along with it was *Isaiah 40:31*: "But they that wait upon the Lord shall renew their strength; they shall mount up with wings as eagles; they shall run, and not be weary; and they shall walk, and not faint."

We put Preston in his wheelchair and walked with the kids to Freedom Park. We were not allowed to put Preston in a vehicle, but no one said we couldn't go on a mile stroll! It was a beautiful, crisp fall day; it did us all a tremendous amount of good to get nature's fresh air.

When we returned from the park, we ordered pizza for the kids. This would be a high-calorie food for Preston, and he still needed extra calories. That night he was able to eat a piece of pizza and laugh with his friends. What an uplifting, magnificently normal sight!

As Preston was improving, the physical therapist taught us how to get Preston in and out of our van. They were going to let us go out on some "weekend passes."

The first pass we got was for a Sunday afternoon. We went to the local mall and pushed Preston in the wheel-chair. He was weak and we didn't stay long. However, it was a welcome change for him and for us. There was an ice skating rink in the middle of the mall, and Patrick was able to skate as we watched. The time together was precious and full of hope.

We took Preston to a store to find his girlfriend a Christmas gift. He found a beautiful sweater with shiny sequins and snowmen on it. He saw it in the window of a store with the same name as his girlfriend. Preston's girlfriend had been faithful to keep in touch by telephone, and she even came to see him a few times. We were thankful for this because he needed support to keep him motivated for the therapy ahead.

Hebrews 12:12–13 tells us, "Wherefore lift up the hands which hang down, and the feeble knees; and make straight paths for your feet, lest that which is lame be turned out of the way; but let it rather be healed."

With his "new personality," we were afraid his girlfriend couldn't accept him as he was. She had known him as the patient, quiet, strong, independent boy he was before. Now he was extremely dependent on us—with a "child-like" faith. He was funny and outspoken with his remarks, and had little patience. It was difficult for us to accept this new behavior, but even more so for her.

We promised God that we would take Preston however He saw fit and be thankful. His girlfriend didn't know the hard times Preston had endured already, and what mountains he still would have to face when he left the center. My husband and I had the unconditional love that only parents can have. I won't say it was easy; we cried many tears over this, also. However, it was a faith-enhancing experience: Imagine the unconditional love our Heavenly Father has for us!

The next Saturday, an activity called "capture the flag" was scheduled for our teens at church. We were both counselors, and we really missed being with our teens. Before the wreck, Preston had been a part of the teen activities. We didn't know if he would even make it to this year's event.

Remarkably, we were given a day pass to go home, but had to return to the hospital that night. The church kids seemed glad to see Preston. He didn't get to participate, but it helped him to associate with the others. How we wished we could all be home for good.

On Sunday, we were able to come home for church for a few hours. It was the first time we had been at a church service in three months. My husband asked one of our teens to sing "He's All I Need" just for me. Christ *is* all we need. It was great to feel the Holy Spirit in our church. God's presence was so thick you could feel it surrounding you and almost see it in the air. *Psalm 31:24* reminds us to "Be of good courage, and He shall strengthen your heart, all ye that hope in the Lord." *I Samuel 22:33* says, "God is my strength and power; and he maketh my way perfect." *Hebrews 10:25* tells us not to forsake "the assembling of ourselves together, as the manner of some is; but exhorting to one another."

Preston continued to make progress. He began "potty training." It was just like when he was first potty trained at the age of two. The nurses would encourage Preston to urinate every two hours. It was difficult for Preston to control his bladder in reference to starting and stopping on command. We would run water in the sink and put his hand in the water. He slowly began to catch on. You don't think about forgetting the necessities of life, but you can! He still had accidents, but we were so proud of any progress.

As Thanksgiving approached, we were learning the true meaning of being thankful—we still had our son! For our family, Thanksgiving isn't just eating turkey and dressing—it's having the family together, loving and being good to each other. Our priorities in life had been reemphasized and reexamined. We also wanted to share the holiday with our extended family, but we didn't know how we would accomplish it.

Again, God made this possible. Preston was allowed to go home for a day visit at Thanksgiving. Our family was ecstatic. We took his medication with us and headed for home. *Home!*

We left Charlotte about 8 a.m. Preston hadn't ridden much lately and he got "carsick." He vomited, but this did not hurt his appetite. He recovered quickly.

When a person has a head injury, they become impulsive about many things. Preston was impulsive about eating and talking. He wanted some food at least every one or two hours, and he talked a lot. Before his accident, he was fairly quiet and shy. Little did we know what was in store for us with this new personality!

Preston had also learned the importance of families and their love for one another. Our extended families had pitched in to help take care of Preston, and he realized how important they were as well as how much they loved all of us.

My husband's family came for Thanksgiving lunch and brought food, and my family came for dinner and brought food. It was delicious. We had a lot of good leftovers to take with us back to Charlotte. I knew Preston would eat well once he had real home cooking.

On Monday after Thanksgiving, the recreational therapist took Preston and the other children on a trip to a pizza parlor, which was located across from the hospital. The object was to stimulate Preston to get back to being a normal teen. Most teens love pizza, and pizza would provide some extra calories for weight gain. The plan was for him to be stimulated to think about what to order and figure out how much money he had to pay for it. He would be encouraged to make decisions about ordering his food. This would foster independence.

It's important to note that when someone suffers a brain injury, that individual needs to be stimulated to use new parts of the brain that have never been used before. The average person uses less than 25 percent of the brain.

Each section of the brain has a different function and the part of Preston's brain that was injured was the frontal lobe, which deals with reasoning and organizational skills. Therefore, he had to be stimulated to learn the basics again. Boy, what things we take for granted!

The doctors informed us that Preston would never be able to perform well in subjects that dealt with reasoning. He would never be organized with his life and everyday activities. But we didn't give up! We knew Christ could do whatever He saw fit, regardless of what the doctors reported. Indeed, if we have faith as small as a mustard seed, God will move mountains.

The week after Thanksgiving was excruciatingly long. After the weekend pass to go home, I was spoiled. I wanted so badly for us to be a family again at our house. The next week, I spent lonely hours at the inn by myself. I managed to occupy myself, but I missed the rest of my family. The hospital added to my injured mood as they wouldn't allow me to be with Preston during the day.

The Father's Hand

While through this changing world below
I would not choose my path to go;
Tis Father's hand that leadeth me,
Then O how safe His child must be.

Sometimes we walk in sunshine bright,
Sometimes in darkness of the night;
Sometimes the way I cannot see
But Father's hand still leadeth me.

Sometimes there seems no way to take,
But Father's hand a way doth make.
Sometimes I hear Him gently say,
"Come follow Me, this is the way."

Why should I mind the way I go?
His way is best for me, I know.
He is my strength, my truth, my way,
He is my comfort, rod, and stay.

So on we travel hand in hand,
Bound for the heavenly promised land
Always through all Eternity,
I'll praise His name for leading me.

—Ida L. Cornett

Meanwhile, Preston was continuing vigorously with his rehabilitation. He was able to go without a diaper now, which was a miracle. Although he still needed a wheelchair on occasion, he was now walking with a cane.

Preston naturally tired very easily and his appetite was still weak. He generally fell asleep for the night by 8 p.m., and it was a triumph to keep him awake until then.

Preston's therapists and doctor had decided to let him go home to stay on Friday, December 4, 1997. Finally, the grand homecoming day was here! God had given us the strength to make it through these awful, trying six weeks at the Charlotte Rehabilitation Center. *Philippians 4:13* declares, "I can do all things through Christ which strengtheneth me."

I believe there's a significance in the number of weeks we were in Charlotte. In the Bible, the number six signifies something evil or related to Satan. Our time in Charlotte had been worse than any "boot camp" I had ever heard of. We had endured these weeks only by the grace of God. Yet with God's help we not only endured them— *we were made stronger!*

The medical staff warned us that life outside the rehabilitation center would be even more exhausting. I didn't quite understand what they meant, but I soon discovered they were right. *Ephesians 5:17* tells us, "Wherefore be ye not unwise, but understanding what the will of the Lord is." God had been with us so far, and we knew He wouldn't leave us now.

Chapter 12
Going Home

Thought for Today

This is the beginning of a new day.
I can waste it or use it for good.
What I do today is important because
I am exchanging a day of my life for it.

When tomorrow comes,
this day will be gone forever—
leaving in its place something I have traded for it.
I want it to be a gain, not loss; good, not evil;
success, not failure; in order that I shall
not regret the price I paid for today.

—Anonymous

Friday, December 4, 1997, finally came and we were headed home! It was the four-year anniversary of my father's death. I knew my father was in heaven watching over us with a smile on his face. I could practically hear him cheering us on. He was so proud of his grandchildren.

I believe the souls of the saints in heaven look down upon us with the deepest concern. *Luke 15:7* affirms: "I say unto you that likewise joy shall be in heaven over one sinner that repenteth." *Hebrews 12:1, 2* states, "wherefore seeing we also compassed about with so great a cloud of witnesses, let us lay aside every weight and the sin which doth so easily beset us, and let us run with patience the race that is set before us, looking unto Jesus the author and finisher of our faith."

This day was one of rejoicing for us. Our family would again be together in our home. Although Preston hadn't fully recovered, he continued to progress. We had our son, and he had us. As we drove north on I-77 toward home, we cried more tears, some falling in our laps and others falling beside us—these were tears of excitement and joy. *We were going home!*

My husband, myself and our two sons—all together—driving up to our home was a dream come true. It was absolute euphoria to be home. Friends from church had built a ramp into the house for Preston to use. My sister-in-law had tied yellow balloons on it to welcome us home.

What a homecoming! It made me think of how sweet heaven will be. Could it be much sweeter than this homecoming day? What a reunion it will be to see our loved ones and Jesus! I cannot comprehend how perfect it will be.

We had waited so long to be a family again, and we had finally made it. We all slept in our own beds, under the same roof.

On Sunday, we went to church together. It was a joy to see our church family again. Our church is so blessed because God always make his presence known there. We were so thankful to be back in this holy place. It's hard to imagine how people exist without Christ. The songs "There is Power in the Blood" and "Victory in Jesus" now had new meaning.

Our first outpatient rehabilitation visit was scheduled for Monday morning. We went three times a week—on Monday, Wednesday and Friday. The weather was chilly on our first outing.

Preston was still having difficulty moving his arms and legs because of increased pain. There was a lot of pain in his joints, his left side being affected the most. He looked like a person recovering from a stroke. This was another mountain to climb.

We met our three therapists who would be in charge of Preston's outpatient rehabilitation. This meant getting acquainted with a new staff. Patients who have had head injuries need to have consistency with everything, so any change was a challenge. We would be with the same therapists for the next nine months.

Preston had to be evaluated by each therapist to see in what areas he needed the most work and help. The evaluation itself made up a long, painful day. Therapy was then scheduled every other day so his body muscles would not forget how to function. The muscles had to be trained how to work properly again.

The body is an amazing machine with everything working together from one central area, the brain. We did some therapy at home, but Preston wouldn't listen to us as well as he did his therapists. It seems that children always listen to others better than their parents!

The Weaver

My life is but a weaving
Between my Lord and me,
I cannot choose the colors
He worketh steadily.

Ofttimes He weaveth sorrow,
And I in foolish pride
Forget He sees the upper
And I, the underside.

Not till the loom is silent
And the shuttles cease to fly
Shall God unroll the canvas
And explain the reason why.

The dark threads are as needful
In the Weaver's skillful hand
As the threads of gold and silver
In the pattern He has planned.

—Grant Colfax Tuller

Chapter 13
School Begins

Preston had been evaluated at Charlotte to check his comprehension level. The results indicated that he was at a third grade level. Imagine how it felt to have a child go from high honor grades to a third grade level. This was a disappointment, but we were thankful to have him alive and at even this level considering the circumstances. We had made a promise to God that we wanted to keep Preston no matter how he was.

We knew we had a laborious road ahead of us to get him back to normal. Doctors said it would take five years to recover to where he was before the accident. As the brain is stimulated, new areas are used, but it was a slow process. Yet Preston worked hard; he refused to give up.

We had a full-time job just taking Preston to Winston-Salem three times a week for therapy. This was exhausting for him, and he would come straight home and nap. He continued to be in bed by 8 o'clock every night.

During this time we could never forget that we had another son who still needed our help and attention. Not only did we have to make sure Patrick had transportation to school and back, but now he needed extra help with homework. Because of the stress, his grades had plunged to almost failing. Fourth grade is an awful transition year anyway. My mother tried to help him, but it had been a long time since she had children of her own in school—schoolwork was harder now.

Patrick's teacher was an angel sent from heaven. She always made extra time for him, and was sensitive to his needs. She worked with us and helped all of us through this difficult time in our lives.

My job was even harder now—I had to be a tutor to Patrick and Preston. I had to continue to make special time with Patrick, and also had to be a wife to David. I reminded myself that God doesn't give us more than we can handle. I did wonder how I could manage these various roles, especially because of my own condition called Chronic Fatigue Immunity Deficiency Syndrome. I knew I couldn't rely on my strength, but must lean completely on Christ. God was the only way I could get through this frantic, demanding schedule.

Preston was scheduled to start back to school after the Christmas holiday. He was scheduled to take an early morning class of drafting at school, and do the other three subjects at home. The medical staff at Charlotte told us that Preston would never have the reasoning skills to do drafting. This made the mountain a little steeper to climb. However, I had the faith that he could do all things through Christ. He had progressed so much already. What an awesome God we serve!

In addition to school, we continued to go to therapy three times a week. I wondered if I could keep up this grueling schedule. Again, I remembered verses from the Bible: *Philippians 4:13:* "I can do all things through Christ which strengtheneth me," and *II Corinthians 12:10*: "for when I am weak, then am I strong." God would sustain me.

In our small school, there had never before been a child with a head injury to the extent of Preston's. The teachers didn't know what was ahead. We were especially afraid of how the other students would treat Preston. Would they accept him?

The Director of Exceptional Children at the County School Board Office was another angel sent to us from above. She helped to get an Individualized Educational Plan (IEP) for Preston. We had never dealt with anything like this, but she helped us through it. The state of North Carolina is required by law to make adaptations for children with learning disabilities, and Preston now fell into this category. Again, God always had a special way of sending special people when we needed them. He is always an "on-time God." Everything always fell into place.

Preston had high anxieties about returning to school. At this time, he was barely able to control his bodily functions. He wasn't sure how people would accept him. Unfortunately, his anxieties were founded. His fears came true! It hurt so badly to see people make fun of him. *How could they ridicule my child?*

Preston's so-called friends deserted him. Other students called him awful names like "retarded," "handicapped," "stupid," and other worse names that I won't repeat. Some people even used curse words, but there were a rare few students who would take up for him. If only these children could understand what he had been through!

Romans 8:16–17 affirms that, "The spirit itself beareth witness with our spirit that we are the children of God. If so be that we suffer with him, that we may be also glorified together." *Romans 8:35, 37* asks us, "Who shall separate us from the love of Christ? Shall tribulation, or distress or persecution, or famine, or nakedness, or peril, or sword? Nay, in all things we are more than conquerors through him that loved us." *Romans 12:19, 21* cautions us, "Dearly beloved, avenge not yourselves, but rather give place unto wrath: for it is written, vengeance is mine; I will repay, saith the Lord. Be not overcome of evil, but overcome evil with good."

As parents, we want to take the pain for our children and intervene in the difficult encounters they have in life. *Oh, how I had wanted to do exactly that ever since the accident.* But we can't always take their pain away or make it better. Only Christ can know what we are going through and wrap His arms around us and make it better.

Since Preston's trials, his two favorite songs became "Under His Wings" and "Redeemed." We would listen to these songs on the way home from school after his morning class, and we could feel the presence of the Holy Spirit in our car as we rode along. In amid this grievous situation, Preston would talk about how God had been so good to him.

Preston told me about a dream he had when he was in his coma. He said he talked to his grandfather in heaven. His grandfather James said it wasn't time for Preston to come to heaven, but he would be waiting on

Preston and his grandfather James on the beach.

him. Even now, just thinking about that dream gives me goose bumps.

A few weeks later, Preston saw his family doctor for a checkup. He had checked in on Preston very faithfully while he was in the hospital, but he was amazed Preston was alive, walking and functioning again. The doctor knew he was seeing a miracle!

As the months progressed, Preston continued working on his schoolwork. When summer came, he had finished his classes with passing grades with God's help. He even passed drafting, the class that the doctors in Charlotte said he would never be able to do. Indeed, we *can* do all things through Christ who strengthens us! *I John 5:4* tells us that "For whatsoever is born of God overcometh the world: and this is the victory that overcometh the world, even the faith."

Preston was progressing very well, and I decided to work part time on his days off from therapy. My mother was able to let him stay with her. It was a hard transition because we had been together nearly nonstop for the last nine months. It brought back memories of carrying him inside me for nine months. Again I felt there was significance in this number. Now it was time for him to be more on his own.

As tough as it was to be apart, I knew it was for his own good. We had to begin reintroducing him back into a normal teen lifestyle.

Preston was apprehensive about me leaving him more. He had to know where I was and when I would be home. He asked my mother these questions several time a day. I missed Preston, but I really needed to work because the bills continued.

Nursing is a demanding field of work, but there are always flexible hours. I was thankful I could return to this job to help support our family financially.

As the summer ended and another school year began, I found myself wondering, *Can I do this juggling act again for another year?* Preston was stronger, and we decided to try letting him stay a full day at school.

His therapy at the rehabilitation center ended because

he was starting school. Our insurance stopped paying some the bills because the state is required to give rehabilitation through the school system. We were able to use the state services provided with speech and occupational therapy. This was the only service we could get because we had applied for financial aid for medical bills and been denied.

My prayer was that Patrick would have a better year. The Lord gave him a very mature, understanding teacher who was very willing to work with him. I was praying he would be back on track this year since we were all together, at home, as a family.

Preston's hardest class to face was U.S. History. The class required lots of memorization and reasoning skills. Preston didn't have the skills required of a normal eleventh grader. He was put in a normal classroom, and was expected to do what the average child could do. He felt terribly defeated. Many nights we both cried over the assignments. My husband works second shift; one night he called home and found us both very upset. He said we would get this problem solved the next day.

We had already talked to his history teacher and guidance counselor to no avail. Neither one understood our situation! His English teacher, who once found me crying in the bathroom because of this situation, did become a good friend to us and was more compassionate about Preston's challenges.

My husband and I called the Director of Exceptional Children in the county. She was compassionate about our problem and wanted to help us. She set up an appointment to get an individualized educational plan (IEP) in place for him. We had to be Preston's lawyer of sorts—his advocate. As parents, we sometimes have to go to bat for our children. Because the state was required to meet his needs, the school provided Preston with his own teacher for this subject. God had answered our prayers yet again!

The second Thanksgiving after the accident came, and it was extra special. After we ate lunch with my mother-in-law, Preston wanted to hit some tennis balls. The weather was good, and he enjoyed the activity a lot. It was good physical therapy for him, although he didn't realize it. I thought, *boy, if the rehabilitation team from Charlotte could see him now!* They wouldn't believe it!

December 17 came and Preston had made it through the first half of the school year with God's help. He had survived the persecution, anxiety and uncertainty with God's mercy and grace. It was draining for him to make it through each school week. By Friday, it was all he could do to drag himself through the day. The second half of the school year started after Christmas vacation; this second half would prove to be less of a challenge mentally as he was steadily improving.

We also got Patrick's report card, and he was making B's and C's! This was a rich blessing for all of us.

Preston's immune system was still weak, and he was constantly sick with various physical problems. I was afraid he would have to deal with this for the rest of his life. He often asked me the question, "Mama, why do I have to live like this?" This broke my heart, but I could not change things. I had to leave it in God's hands and continue to pray.

Preston continued to excel in his Christian work at church. We encouraged him to keep Christ first in his life. The Holy Spirit also helped him keep his focus in the right direction. He was again active in Proteens. The church youth group's activities included reading scripture, doing daily devotions and applying practical Christian work in their lives. Preston was not only able to catch up with the other teens, but was ranked third in about 25 teen-agers in his performance. *II Timothy 2:15* reminds us to "study to show thyself approved unto God, a workman that needeth not to be ashamed, rightly dividing the word of truth." Preston was doing exactly that and we were extremely proud of him.

His Yoke is Easy

A man was carrying a heavy basket.
His son asked to help him. The father cut a stick
and placed it through the handle of the basket
so that the end toward himself was very short,
while the end toward the boy was three or four
times as long. Each took hold of his end of the
stick, and the basket was lifted and easily carried.
The son was bearing the burden with the father,
but he found his work easy and light because
his father assumed the heavy end of the stick.
Just so it is when we bear the yoke with Christ;
He sees to it that the burden laid on us is light;
He carries the heavy end.

—John T. Faris

Chapter 14
What Does the Future Hold?

May 21, 1999: Another school year ended, and Preston was able to graduate with his class. What a milestone he had reached! He looked so handsome in his cap and gown, and we were so proud of him. We had been there for Preston through the valleys and up the mountains and knew what trials he had faced, but not like God. Only God knew exactly what Preston had been through, and what a successful event this was.

The senior class practiced the morning of graduation. My face was washed with tears as I watched them practice. *How would I react at the real graduation?* I was overcome with how much God had blessed my child.

Graduation night was one of the biggest events of our family life. I got to school early and saved a whole row of seats for our family. Preston received an unexpected award from the faculty called the "Danforth Award," which was given to students who had faced tremendous obstacles during their high school years. Preston also graduated with honors. He had advanced from a third grade level in Charlotte to this.

God had worked a miracle in Preston. He gave Preston the strength and courage to go forward with his life. His earthly friends forsook him, but God never did. What an awesome God we serve! He truly is the "Master Physician." We can't praise Him enough for his goodness and mercy.

I don't know what the future holds for Preston, but I know God will never fail him. Preston still has problems with organizational skills and insecurity. His family will be there for him no matter what mountains may come into his path.

Preston is scheduled to go to a technical college this fall. I pray he can learn a vocation and find a satisfying job. We trust this will be yet another new beginning in his life. His new friends can accept him for who he is now. We firmly believe God will use Preston's testimony in a special way to show others what an awesome God He is. Wherever the Lord leads Preston, I hope he will follow. *I Peter 1:7* states, "That the trial of your faith, being much more precious than of gold that perisheth, though it be tried with fire, might be found unto praise and honor and glory at the appearing of Jesus Christ."

A Prayer from a Teen-Ager

O God, help make me a better kid. Help me love my parents like I should. Help me understand that just because they don't give me everything I ask for, it doesn't mean they don't love me. In my heart, I know it means they love me enough to say "no."

May I always believe that my parents do the best they can. Help me not to compare what they do for me with what they do for my brothers and sisters. Sometimes, I need to be reminded that we are all individuals with different needs.

Give me the good sense to accept criticism from my parents without losing my cool. They have been around a lot longer than I have and know what is best for me.

Help me, Lord, not to blow up when my parents ask me where I'm going or when I will be home. They aren't being nosy. They really care.

Help me to be patient and answer their questions without putting them down. They grew up in a different era and many things about our culture are strange to them.

Especially, Dear Lord, help me to respect them. They aren't perfect, but neither am I. Help me to be courteous to them. It's funny how we treat the people closest to us with a lot less respect than we give strangers.

Finally, God, bless my parents for all the things they do for me, and help me love them as much as they love me.

Afterword

If anyone in your family has a similar problem, I hope this book has helped and encouraged you. Please recommend it to others you meet with similar obstacles.

There are many support groups to help you. There's a state association with local chapters for patients with traumatic brain injuries. Please refer to this book's resource appendix for additional assistance. Also, talk with and listen to traumatic brain injury victims, and let them pour out their hearts to you. They, too, felt like they were at the end of the world. They'll tell you how hard they fought to return to a normal daily life. They'll tell you of the extremely difficult and seemingly impossible therapies they endured. They'll tell you of the many, many times they were ready to give up; but through the encouragement of family and friends and with God's loving hand, they managed to overcome most of their difficulties resulting from their injuries.

Doctors say it takes up to five years to get over a brain injury. We have more than two years behind us now. Please continue to pray for us to grow in Christ and face the trials ahead. We will pray for you if you'll contact us.

If you don't know our Savior as the Lord of your life, I encourage you to make that decision. He is the greatest friend you will ever have!

Romans 3:23 states, "For all have sinned, and come short of the glory of God." *Romans 6:23* says, "For the wages of sin is death, but the gift of God is eternal life through Jesus Christ our Lord." *Romans 5:8* reminds us, "But God commendeth his love toward us, in that, while we were yet sinners, Christ died for us." *Romans 10:13* declares, "For whosoever shall call upon the name of the Lord shall be saved." This is a simple plan isn't it? I encourage you to make this decision. It will change your life. It's the most important decision you can ever make.

Psalm 18:2–3 tells us "The Lord is my rock, and my fortress, and my deliverer; My God, my strength, in whom I will trust. I will call upon the Lord, who is worthy to be praised." This was truly an answered prayer for my family.

We still face deep valleys, but we know God will never leave nor forsake us. Every mountain has its valleys, and we have learned the best route to the top is always along these valleys. Some of them may be exceedingly dark and lonely ones. In all of our lives there will be specific valleys to cross. It doesn't matter the number of valleys or whether they're very dark or dimly shadowed ones. If we have the good Shepherd in our lives, we can face any calamity with the assurance that His gracious spirit will guide us and help us face them fearlessly.

Hebrews 13:5 gloriously reminds us, "I will never leave thee nor forsake thee." *Psalm 46:1* tells us, "God is our refuge and strength, a very present help in trouble." God has proven Himself true and faithful to us over and over again, and I know He will be faithful to you, also, if you will let Him. We thank Him for the miracles performed in our lives. To God be the glory. *Bless His name!*

Resources Appendix

1. Winston-Salem Area Family Support Group:
Our closest support group that works with BGSM is with Diane Rankin (336-621-2764); it meets every third Tuesday from 6:30 p.m.–8 p.m. Bowman Gray School of Medicine (www.bgsm.edu/bgsm/surg–sci/ns/trauma.html). Any rehabilitation center can direct you to your closest support group.

2. N.C. Brain Injury Family Help Line:
1-800-377-1464 or online at www.bianc.org.

3. Traumatic Brain Injury (TBI):
Supplies information, support and products for people caring for a loved one at home with a traumatic brain injury (http://www.webofcare.com/TBI).

4. TRI Online Support Groups—Head Injury:
Provides resources to promote independent living services for people with disabilities, parent advocacy and benefits (www.idsi.net/tri/arts.htm).

5. TBI/Net/Aboutus:
Started by John and Clara Lyon in late 1997. They started it as both victim and caregiver when Clara was in a motor vehicle accident and her husband had to care for her (http://tbi.org/whohtm).

6. Brain Injury Society:
Serves individuals and their families; contains online

newsletters and events (www.virtualtrialls.com/bis).

7. TBI Support Group:
Offers awareness, information, resources, opportunity, advocacy and emotional support (www.resctr.org/tbi.html).

8. National Head Injury Foundation:
1-800-444-6443.

9. Traumatic Brain Injury LAW:
Offers free advice from attorneys who specialize in TBI cases (www.freeadvice.com/law/633us.htm).

10. Mild Traumatic Brain Injury:
Helps plead TBI court cases. Most TBI's lead to some kind of permanent disability that would deserve social security benefits or insurance settlements (www.cle.bc.ca/bookstore/mildbrain.htm).

11. Optometric Extension Program (OEP):
Deals with vision-related problems (www.healthy.net/OEP/BRAIN/htm).

12. N.C. Vocational Rehabilitation:
Area contact–Mr. Lloyd Rollins, 1372 Highway 601 South, Mocksville, NC 27028 or call 336-751-0558.

13. Local Mental Health Agencies:
Contact agencies in your area. Local, state-supported programs are in place to help you. These services can range from having people stay with your loved one or helping to pay for medications.

14. Local Board of Education:
Boards of Education have someone who deals with special needs for school children. The main way in which he or she can help a child with a brain injury is in developing an implementing an individualized education plan (IEP) for each child. This person can also help educate parents about parental rights.

15. NICHCY or "Kids' Source Online":
Information related to TBI in children (http://ws1.kidssource.com/NICHCY/brain.html).

16. Family Education:
Deals with families coping with a loved one who has a TBI (www.familyeducation.com).

17. WRAMC AASC Traumatic Brain Injury Program:
General information about TBI available through Walter Reid Hospital.

18. Easter Seals:
Call 1-800-221-6827 for local chapter information.

19. Cerebral Remediation for Traumatic Brain Injury:
Provides general information. Call 1-800-992-6122.

20. Living Life After a Brain Injury:
Helps people to cope with everyday problems (www.biausa.org/living//htm).

Any of this information can be sent to you at no cost.
These agencies understand the impact of a TBI on families.

To order additional copies of

Strength to Climb the Mountains

contact Margaret Harrison at
1141 Hoots Road
Yadkinville, North Carolina 27055